T0273355

THE LITTLE BOOK ABOUT

ICE CREAM

Published in 2022 by OH!
An Imprint of Welbeck Non-Fiction Limited,
part of Welbeck Publishing Group.
Based in London and Sydney.
www.welbeckpublishing.com

Compilation text © Welbeck Non-Fiction Limited 2022
Design © Welbeck Non-Fiction Limited 2022

Disclaimer:
This book is intended for general informational purposes only and should not be relied upon as recommending or promoting any specific practice, diet or method of treatment. It is not intended to diagnose, advise, treat or prevent any illness or condition and is not a substitute for advice from a professional practitioner of the subject matter contained in this book. You should not use the information in this book as a substitute for medication, nutritional, diet, spiritual or other treatment that is prescribed by your practitioner. The publisher makes no representations or warranties with respect to the accuracy, completeness or currency of the contents of this work, and specifically disclaim, without limitation, any implied warranties of merchantability or fitness for a particular purpose and any injury, illness, damage, death, liability or loss incurred, directly or indirectly from the use or application of any of the contents of this book. Furthermore, the publisher is not affiliated with and does not sponsor or endorse any uses of or beliefs about in any way referred in this book.

All rights reserved. No part of this publication may be reproduced, stored in a retrieval system, or transmitted in any form or by any means (including electronic, mechanical, photocopying, recording, or otherwise) without prior written permission from the publisher.

ISBN 978-1-80069-032-5

Compiled and written by: Malcolm Croft
Editorial: Victoria Godden
Project manager: Russell Porter
Design: James Pople
Production: Jess Brisley

A CIP catalogue record for this book is available from the British Library

Printed in China

10 9 8 7 6 5 4 3 2 1

Illustrations: Freepik.com

THE LITTLE BOOK ABOUT

ICE CREAM

FROZEN TO PERFECTION

CONTENTS

INTRODUCTION

Welcome to the bowl-licking, cone-dripping, sticky-fingering world of all that is incredible about ice cream. Today, humankind's passion for ice cream comes in hundreds-and-thousands of shapes and sizes, sprinkles and spoonful's, splits and sundaes, with more flavours to choose from than you can shake an ice cream scoop at. Yes, ice cream is arguably the greatest thing to happen to us since bread came sliced, which was actually invented after ice cream, but you get the picture.

So, to celebrate all that is sweet and dreamy about ice cream, this tiny tome is the inside scoop of how divine ice cream has become to us mortals. *The Little Book About Ice Cream* is the ultimate book-shaped party of all things nice (and naughty) about ice cream in all its gloriously indulgent forms – a bedside cone-panion, if you will, for when you need a little pick-me-up.

So, pick up your spoon (or two), scoop a scoop (or three) and don't forget to pop your cherry on top – because you're about to be spoiled rotten. Tuck in...

CHAPTER
ONE

Inside Scoop

I scream, you scream, we all scream for ice cream. With that phrase as our guiding light, let us go now on a quest of delicious self-discovery and scoff as much ice cream-flavoured information as we can into our minds before we get brain freeze. Little wooden spoons at the ready... Here we go...

"

Dear frozen yogurt, you are the celery of desserts. Be ice cream, or be nothing.

"

Ron Swanson,
Parks and Recreation,
Season 6, Episode 14: "Anniversaries"

66

Now put your clothes back on, and I'll buy you an ice cream.

99

James Bond (Daniel Craig),
Casino Royale, **2006**

**Beyoncé is the dairy
queen of ice cream.**

She loves it.
Her favourite flavour?

Butter pecan.

Ice Queen

The Royal Family is not exempt from having sweet teeth. Queen Elizabeth II is fond of licking the plate clean when served a Bombe Glacée Royale, her decadent dessert of choice. What is it? Put simply: it's a mint ice cream cannonball filled with chocolate on a bed of whipped cream. This regal indulgence was served at the Queen's wedding to Prince Philip in 1947.

The Nazis surrendered at 11.01pm on May 8, 1945, effectively bringing an end to World War II. To celebrate the victory – and because dairy product rationing was immediately jettisoned – Americans ate ice cream. A lot. So much so, they effectively established the summer craze for eating ice cream. By 1946, the average American had consumed 35 pints of ice cream each – a record yet to be beaten.

At a G20 summit in 2009,
Queen Elizabeth once asked
her husband Prince Philip why
the Italian president, Silvio
Berlusconi, had to talk so loudly.
Prince Philip replied rudely
(as he often would):
**"He is Italian, my dear, how
else would he sell his ice
creams?"**

Three gallons (24 pints) of whole milk are required to make just one gallon (8 pints) of ice cream. Thankfully, a cow produces more than 2,300 gallons each year, equivalent to 350,000 glasses of milk in a lifetime.

There are two schools of thought when making modern mass-produced ice cream:

1. French Style

made with eggs, so it's thick and custardy.

2. Philadelphia/ American Style

made with sugar, milk and cream, so it's lighter and fluffy.

Vanilla Ice's favourite ice cream flavour is not vanilla.*

*Probably

The world's first American waffle cone
for ice cream was created – apparently – at
the 1904 St. Louis World's Fair by a Syrian
waffle-maker named Ernest A. Hamwi –
more by luck than judgement. Hamwi was
selling his *zalabis* – a crispy, waffle pastry
– in a booth opposite an ice cream vendor.
When the ice cream vendor ran out of
paper bowls, Hamwi rolled a zalabis in the
shape of a horn – a cornucopia* – and gave
it to him. The waffle cone was born.

* The word "cone" comes from 'Cornucopia', an ornamental
horn of plenty: a horn-shaped container overflowing with
fruits, and flowers, a traditional gift to express prosperity.

According to Dairy Press Room in California (the U.S.'s largest ice cream producer, FYI), 64 per cent of ice cream consumers in the U.S. eat their ice cream in front of the TV. Nineteen per cent of Americans take it to the bedroom.*

* Three per cent also admitted they often eat ice cream in the bathtub. Heroes.

During WWII, on June 24, 1942, a Japanese warship torpedoed the U.S.S. *Lexington*, the second-largest aircraft carrier in the U.S. Navy, in the Pacific. Before the 3,000 crewmembers evacuated via lifeboats, they devoured the ice cream onboard by scooping it into their helmets, unsure of when they'd eat again. Some 216 crew were killed that day, and 2,735 were rescued.

Penny Lick

In late-nineteenth-century London street vendors sold ice cream... by the lick! A Penny Lick was a small glass filled with ice cream. Passing customers would lick a shot of ice cream and return the glass to the vendor. Who would then reuse it. *Without washing it*.

Sensibly, the Penny Lick was outlawed in 1898, after outbreaks of cholera and tuberculosis.

The first recorded recipe for an ice cream cone appears in Agnes Marshall's *Mrs Marshall's Cookery Book*, published in 1888. Apparently, Mrs Marshall so loathed the unsanitary "Penny Lick" culture in London that she devised a pastry cone to allow a more hygienic approach to eating ice cream on the go.

In a survey conducted
by Baskin Robbins,
1 in 10 ice cream lovers
lick the bowl clean.

Are you the one?

Marge, our marriage is like soft-serve ice cream. And trust is the hard chocolate shell that keeps it from melting onto our carpet. In 'cone-clusion' here's the scoop: I love you.

Homer Simpson, *The Simpsons*,
Season 18, Episode 8: "Ice Cream of Margie"

Ice Cream Playlist: Ice Cream

"Ice Cream" – Selena Gomez
"Ice Cream Man" – Blur
"Ice Cream Cakes" – Jeff Beck Group
"Ice Cream Party" – Modest Mouse
"Ice Cream" – Sarah McLachlan
"Ice Cream Girl" – Lloyd Cole
"Ice Cream Van" – Glasvegas
"Ice Cream Man" – Van Halen
"Ice Cream Cake" – Red Velvet
"Ice Cream Castles" – The Time
"Ice Cream Truck" – Beyoncé

And one more just to be different...
"Spoonman" – Soundgarden

66

Lisa, don't you like ice cream better when it's covered in hot fudge... and mounds of whipped cream... choc nuts, and those crumpled up cookie things they put on top? Mmmmcrumpled up cookie things.

99

Homer Simpson, *The Simpsons*, Episode: 'Lisa the Greek'

Why did the ice cream van break down?

Because of the Rocky Road.*

*Sorry

66

The only good
thing about being
wounded in the
buttocks... is the
ice cream.

99

Forrest Gump, *Forrest Gump*, 1994

Icons of Ice Cream: #1

Ben & Jerry's was founded by childhood friends Ben Cohen and Jerry Greenfield in 1978 in Burlington, Vermont. B&J are famous for releasing popular-culture flavoured ice creams, such as "Scotchy Scotch Scotch" – a butterscotch flavour ice cream inspired by the classic Will Ferrell movie, *Anchorman: The Legend of Ron Burgundy*.

Super Scooper

In honour of all the bent spoons out there, let us bow our heads and pay respect to Alfred L. Cralle - the inventor of the ice cream scoop!

Cralle patented the scoop in 1897, and called it an "Ice Cream Mold and Disher", after he noticed that ice cream rather annoyingly stuck to the spoons servers used in restaurants.

The word **"scoop"** dates back to the 14th century, originally employed by the Dutch to refer to a bucket. The first recorded usage of the word dates back to 1338, in Arthurian legend: a young Merlin tells King Vortigern that in order to find two dragons in an underground pool beneath his fortress, he'll need to "scoop" out the water.

"

When you start
getting screwed over
all the time, you gotta
switch to low fat.

"

**Monica Gellar, *Friends*,
Season 3, Episode 4: "The One With the
Metaphorical Tunnel"**

Dish Fit For (Only) a King

On St. George's Day, in 1671, at a lavish ceremonial banquet at Windsor Castle, the first recorded serving of ice cream in England was observed. The guests at King Charles II's table were the only ones allowed to eat the cherished dish, "One plate of white strawberries and one plate of ice cream".

It is estimated that
to finish one large
scoop of ice cream
(in an ice cream cone)
requires 50 licks.
Don't believe us?
Go count.
No cheating!

Ice Cream Nations

According to a 2021 report by IndexBox, the 15 countries listed are the top exporters of the world's ice cream:

Germany (13.7% - also the top importer)
France (12.7%)
Belgium (9.6%)
Netherlands (7.8%)
Italy (6.2%)
United States (5.8%)
Poland (5.5%)

United Kingdom (3.9%)
Hungary (3.2%)
Spain (2.9%)
Thailand (2%)
Slovenia (1.8%)
South Korea (1.4%)
Sweden (1.4%)
Russia (1.3%)

Ice Cream Playlist: Rated PG

"Sweet Dreams" – Eurythmics
"Ice Cream Soda" –
The White Stripes
"Cold As Ice" – Foreigner
"Ice Baby" – Vanilla Ice
"Ice In the Sun" – Status Quo
"A Chocolate Sundae on a Saturday
Night" – Doris Day
"Hot Fudge" – Robbie Williams
"Drip" – Cardi B
"Sticky Sweet" – Motley Crue
"I Want a Little Sugar
In My Bowl" – Nina Simone

CHAPTER
TWO

Ice Ice Baby

Ice cream is as tasty as it is teachy. Since the industrial revolution, when ice cream became the hot new thing in town, it has inspired a plethora of movie-makers, authors, artists, philosophers and scientists – everyone from Einstein to Kardashian – to melt for its dreamy, creamy charms. Everyone is talking about ice cream... are you?

Ice cream loses its soft and fluffy feel after being repeatedly thawed and refrozen. The millions of microscopic air bubbles that keep the ice cream soft and fluffy escape each time the ice cream thaws, and the molecular structure breaks down further. So, your ice cream becomes tougher and less fluffy with each visit to the freezer.

Every week day, Ben & Jerry's employees are permitted to take any three tubs of ice cream home with them they wish. The company employs more than 1,000 staff.

Brain Freeze

Pleasure is nothing without a little pain, right? If (sorry, *when*) you eat ice cream a bit too quickly, the blood vessels that connect your mouth to your brain restrict and trap the blood flow momentarily.

This triggers the trigeminal nerve that carries sensory information from your face around your head into a mini-meltdown.

Don't panic: if you press your tongue against the roof of your mouth, this should warm those vessels back up.

Sundae Yummy Sundae

The genesis of ice cream sundaes came about in 1890, when religious law-makers in Evanston, Illinois, made it illegal to sell ice cream sodas on Sunday, the Day of their Lord, Sunday. Local ice cream capitalists looped around the law by replacing soda with syrup instead, and renamed it an "Ice Cream Sunday". The Y was replaced with an E to appease religious leaders. And so the sundae was born again.

Seal of Approval

Thomas Jefferson, the U.S.'s third president (1801–1809), is credited as the first American to write down an ice cream recipe (vanilla, naturally), and helped popularize the expansion of ice cream across the nation. He would serve it regularly at the White House. The president first tasted ice cream during his time in France (1784–1789).

The modern translation of his recipe, reads:

"Beat the yolks of 6 eggs until thick and lemon coloured. Add, gradually, 1 cup of sugar and a pinch of salt. Bring to a boil 1 quart of cream and pour slowly on the egg mixture. Put in top of double boiler and when it thickens, remove and strain through a fine sieve into a bowl. When cool add 2 teaspoonfuls of vanilla. Freeze, as usual, with one part of salt to three parts of ice. Place in a mould, pack in ice and salt for several hours. For electric refrigerators, follow usual direction, but stir frequently."

Thomas Jefferson

Ben, from Ben & Jerry's, has anosmia. He is unable to smell or taste his own ice cream. This is why B&J's specialize in funky-flavoured chunky ice creams – the lumps give Ben a texture to at least chew on.

Published in 1558, Neapolitan chemist Giambattista Della Porta's *Magia Naturalis* was the first book to describe the earliest techniques for freezing liquids, now known as the Endothermic Process.

Porta's discovery was simple, but alchemic: by immersing ice or water in snow with saltpetre* (the explosive ingredient in gunpowder!), a liquid will rapidly turn to ice. Add sugar, eggs and cream... and... well, you've got a party.

*Any old salt will do, he discovered with a bang.

"

I walked into Cartwright's and ordered two coffee ice cream sodas – to steady my nerves. A man, I suppose, would have had a stiff peg; but girls derive a lot of comfort from ice cream sodas. I applied myself to the end of the straw with gusto. The cool liquid went trickling down my throat in the most agreeable manner. I pushed the first glass aside empty.

"

Agatha Christie

66

Don't be a leader if you want to make everyone happy; instead, sell ice cream!

99

Steve Jobs

"

In the meantime, for elegance and ease and luxury, the Hattons and Milles' dine here to-day, and I shall eat ice and drink French wine, and be above vulgar economy.

"

Jane Austen (in letters to Cassandra, Godmersham, June 20, 1808)

> We do not get ice cream everywhere, and so, when we do, we are apt to dissipate to excess.

Mark Twain

In 2006, the world's first proper (non-freeze-dried) ice cream was eaten in space when Space Shuttle Atlantis delivered a freezer to be installed on the space station. NASA decided to pack it with pints of Blue Bell brand ice cream. In 2017, SpaceX's Dragon capsule delivered Blue Bell's ice cream once again, as is now the tradition. Three flavour choices were launched: chocolate, vanilla and birthday-cake.

"

Such ice cream I would not
trade for a steak and kidney
pudding, a boiled silversmith
with carrots & dumplings, or a
Kentish chicken pudding.
In fact, I like it.

"

**Alfred Hitchcock
(on the beauty of American ice cream)**

"

You cannot defeat a nation that enjoys ice cream at -40°C.

"

Winston Churchill (on Russia)

Albert Einstein's love for ice cream is as famous as his $E = MC^2$. Upon arriving in Princeton, New York, where he became a tenured professor during World War II, Einstein's first shop-stop was to buy an American ice cream. At the Baltimore ice cream parlour on Nassau Street, he ordered vanilla ice cream with chocolate sprinkles. The server, John Lampe, watched Einstein take hold of his ice cream: "The great man looked at the cone, smiled at me...and pointed his thumb first at the cone and then at himself," Lampe recalled.

Elvis Presley had a notoriously sweet tooth. Apart from his infamous fondness for a bacon-laden Fools' Gold Loaf, the King also had a penchant for ice cream. Chocolate milkshake and peach = were the flavours that

got him all shook up.

According to the Guinness World Records, the world's largest ever ice cream sundae weighed 24.91 tonnes (54,917 lb) – the same weight as a fire engine. The sundae was made by Palm Dairies, in Edmonton, Alberta, Canada on July, 24 1988 – a Sunday.

In 1986, an ice cream fan anonymously posted the idea for "Cherry Garcia" flavour ice cream on a board at her local B&J scoop shop. The idea went unnoticed. The fan persisted with a follow-up postcard that read:

"Dear Ben & Jerry's, We're great fans of the Grateful Dead and we're great fans of your ice cream. Why don't you make a cherry flavour and call it Cherry Garcia? You know it will sell because Dead paraphernalia

always sells. We are talking good business sense here, plus it will be a real hoot for the fans."

The company listened. Cherry Garcia received its first lick in public on February 15, 1987. It now endures as one of the brand's bestselling flavours. Several months later, Ben and Jerry received a note: "I'm glad you made the flavour." It was signed by Jane Williamson, the no-longer anonymous muse behind Cherry Garcia.

Spilt Milk

According to Greek mythology, our galaxy – the Milky Way – is named so because Zeus's wife, Hera, spilt several drops of breastmilk onto the night sky while giving birth to her son, Hercules. The term "Milky Way" derives from the Greek "milky circle".

The presence of phosphorus in ice cream increases a person's libido by boosting testosterone levels. Ergo, the more ice cream you eat, the more sexually carnivorous you feel.*

*Paradoxically, most doctors would not recommend having vigorous sex immediately after eating a ton of ice cream.

For an ice cream to be called "dairy ice cream" it must legally contain a minimum of 10 per cent milkfat. Most premium ice cream contains 12 to 15 per cent. Soft-serve ice cream contains no more than 6 per cent, often just 3.

According to Talking Retail, the Covid-19 pandemic led to a 22 per cent increase in global ice cream sales in 2020, with worldwide premium ice cream sales increasing by 50 per cent. So, in the middle of a pandemic, ice cream lovers wanted two things:

1. *Better ice cream.*

2. *Lots more of it.*

66

Ice cream is my weakness. If I could eat whatever I wanted every day I would have Domino's Pizza with pasta carbonara inside every slice. And, at night, I would have Neapolitan ice cream until I felt absolutely toxic. And then I would drift off telling myself, *It's gonna be okay. It's gonna be okay. You're gonna train in the morning.*

99

Robert Downey Jr.

In 2021, Ben & Jerry's was the leading brand of ice cream in the U.S. The company sold **202 million tubs**, or **$936 million dollars'** worth. That's what we call devotion to dessert.

66

Häagen-Dazs is my biggest indulgence. Their dulce de leche flavour is my favourite thing in life.

99

Kim Kardashian

"

Life is like an
ice-cream cone,
you have to lick it
one day at a time.

"

Charles M. Schulz

> **"**
>
> # Ice-cream is exquisite – what a pity it isn't illegal.
>
> **"**

Voltaire

66

It's never too early for ice cream.

99

Michael Scott (Steve Carrell),
The Office (U.S.)

66

It is a grave error to assume that ice cream consumption requires hot weather.

99

Anne Fadiman

Proclamation No. 5219

In 1984, President Ronald Reagan decreed every third Sunday of July, and the month in general, to be all about ice cream. On that day National Ice Cream Day (and Month) became an institution as American as, well, apple pie.

The proclamation – no. 5219 – stated: "Ice cream is a nutritious and wholesome food enjoyed by over ninety percent of the people in the United States."

So, there, it's official.

Ice Cream Playlist: Rated R

These songs don't suck...they lick.

"Just Don't Bite It" – N.W.A.
"Get My Licks"– Isley Brothers
"Licking Stick"– James Brown
"Pour Some Sugar On Me" –
Def Leppard
"Milkshake" – Kelis
"Lick It Before You Stick It" –
Denise LaSalle
"How Many Licks" – Lil Kim
"Suck It and See" – Arctic Monkeys
"Whip It" – Devo
"Milk It" – Nirvana

According to the USDA, a plain scoop of vanilla ice cream energizes your body to the tune of 140 calories. To burn this off, you'll need to run for 20 minutes.

Anything But Vanilla

There are thousands of wonderful and weird flavours of ice cream in the world today. However, vanilla remains the world's most popular flavour. Its existence is anything but ordinary...

1. Vanilla is the only edible fruit of the orchid family of 25,000 different species.

2. The vanilla flower blooms for 24 hours and must be pollinated or dies.

3. A stick, the size of a toothpick is used to hand-pollinate the vanilla beans.

4. Vanilla is extracted from the cured pods (beans) of the orchid flowers from vanilla vines.

5. Vanilla is found, predominately, in Sava, Madagascar. The region supplies 75 per cent of all the world's vanilla.

6. Vanilla translates to "little pod" in Spanish.

7. Vanilla is anything but vanilla – it has more than 500 different flavour and fragrance components.

8. Vanilla is the second most expensive spice in the world (after saffron).

9. 99 per cent of vanilla-flavoured products on the market don't contain any vanilla (just synthesized vanilla).

10. Synthesized vanilla can be made from the anal glands of beavers.

CHAPTER
THREE

Cream of the Crop

There's something about ice cream that just makes people feel good. But why? Is it the creamy fluffiness? Or the swirly sauciness? Or is it the chunky chewiness? Step right up for more ice cream-inspired wit, wisdom and wisecracks. Try not to over-indulge!

It was renowned ice cream obsessive, President Thomas Jefferson, who, in 1789, was the first American to bring 200 vanilla beans to the continental United States (as well as his famous ice cream recipe) following his role as Ambassador to France. Until then, chocolate and fruit were more commonly used to flavour ice cream.

Today, the United States is the single largest consumer of vanilla in the world.

> In the days of the monarchy in Italy, the King had a specifically chosen guard consisting of 99 men, and subsequently anything really special or first class was known as '99' – and that is how '99' Flake came by its name.

So says Cadbury, the Flake-maker (there are many rumours contrary to this)

Best Job in the World

The world's best known food taster has to be John Harrison, who was employed by world-famous ice cream maker Dreyer's. Throughout his "career" (is ice cream tasting a career?), Harrison claimed he tasted a "few hundred million gallons of ice cream". His taste-testing skills were so valuable that Dreyer's insured his tongue for $1 million. He was also the creator of cookies-and-cream flavoured ice cream.

Rocky Road

In 1929, William Dreyer and Joseph Edy invented Rocky Road ice cream. Today, it is one of the most popular ice cream flavours ever. Legend tells us that Dreyer added cut-up nuts to a bowl of ice cream that he snipped with his wife's sewing scissors. He called it Rocky Road "to give folks something to smile about in the midst of the Great Depression," said Dreyer following the Wall Street Crash of 1929.

Transfer ice cream to
the refrigerator for
10 minutes before serving.
This ensures ice cream is
soft enough to serve without
thawing enough to ruin it.
**Ice cream scientists agree,
the perfect temperature
for scooping ice cream is
between 6º (–14ºC)
and 10ºF (–12ºC).**

In 1943, American heavy
bomber aircraft crews devised
a cunning way to make ice
cream onboard their airplanes.
They strapped buckets of ice
cream mix (a vital ration for all
military personnel) at the back
of the plane, by the tail gunners'
autocannon. By the time they
had landed, the mix had frozen
at altitude and been churned
smooth by engine vibrations,
turbulence and extreme
flight maneuverers.

Häagen-Dazs

The ice cream brand name, Häagen-Dazs, doesn't mean anything. Neither does the umlaut. The name is a creation of Reuben Mattus, who founded the brand with his wife, Rose, and wanted something – anything – "Danish-sounding". It's not Danish.

Mattus' daughter Doris recalled how her father would "sit at the kitchen table for hours saying nonsensical words until he came up with a combination he liked."

During the U.S. Prohibition era (1920–1929) ice cream sales rose by more than 40 per cent. The most powerful lobby for Prohibition, the Anti-Saloon League, told the world in 1921: **"It is believed that this large increase in ice cream consumption was due in a large degree to the fact that men with a craving for stimulants turned readily to this refreshing and palatable food."**

Former British Prime Minister, and Iron Lady, Margaret Thatcher did not invent soft-serve ice cream, as Google tries to teach us. However, she was a food research scientist at J. Lyons ice cream manufacturer before entering politics. Thatcher reportedly worked on the quality of cake and pie fillings as well as on ice cream. Her favourite flavour is a state secret. (Ice cream is also a poor source of iron.)

Approximately, 2,500 years
ago, during Tang Dynasty
China ice cream was made
by freezing a mixture of rice
and milk in snow. Marco Polo,
the great Venetian explorer,
witnessed this process during
his travels there and is said to
have introduced this "sherbet"
to Italy, hence why most people
assume ice cream is an
Italian invention.

1 in 10 people admit to licking the bowl clean after eating ice cream.

Viagra Ice Cream

In 2014, Charlie Harry Francis, founder of the famous Lick Me I'm Delicious ice cream brand, was the first (but definitely not the last) to make an ice cream mixed with Viagra, the erection-erecting pill. The flavour, called Arousal, contains 25 milligrams of Viagra and comes in one colour – blue, like the pill.

To Make Icy Cream

"Take three pints of the best cream, boyle it with a blade of Mace or else perfume it with orang flower water or Amber Greece, sweeten the Cream, with sugar let it stand till it is quite cold, then put it into Boxes, ether of Silver or tinn, then take, Ice chopped into small peeces and put it into a tub and set the Boxes in the Ice covering them all over, and let them stand in the Ice two hours,

and the Cream Will come to be Ice in the Boxes, then turn them out into a salvar with some of the same seasoned Cream, so sarve it up to the Table."

This is Lady Anne Fanshawe's ice cream recipe. She was an English noblewoman. It is believed to be the first published ice cream recipe in history, published circa 1668.

By law in the UK, ice cream vans are not permitted to play their Pied Piper-esque chimes before 12 noon and after 7pm. The English Code of Practice on "Noise from Ice-cream vans chimes" of 1982 states that it is illegal to sound ice cream van chimes at certain times and locations. To do so is an annoyance. The law is loud and clear:

- not to be sounded for any longer than four seconds at a time

- not to be used more than once every three minutes

- not to be used near other ice cream vans trading nearby

- not to be sounded when stationary

- not to be sounded within 50 metres of schools, places of worship or hospitals

- not to be used more than once every two hours in the same street

Ice Cream Wars

In Scotland during the 1980s, rival gangs started selling drugs and stolen goods from ice cream vans. The battle for territory between the two criminal organizations became known as the Ice Cream Wars. The Strathclyde Police, who were unable to control the increasing violence between the two sides, were nicknamed the "Serious Chimes Squad" by the local community, a pun on Serious Crime Squad.

On average, **48 ice cream sandwiches*** – ice cream sandwiched between two oatmeal cookies – are devoured *every second* in the United States.

*The best way to make ice cream sandwiches, FYI, is to saw an inch-thick slice off the top of a frozen tub. It offers the perfect cylindrical shape for the cookie!

Next time you're at a child's birthday party and ice cream is served, why not offer up this fact to sound clever...

Ice cream is a foam *and* an emulsion!

(Ice cream is only ever partly frozen as the majority of the space is occupied by air bubbles and ice crystals.)

Neapolitan ice cream was the first ice cream to combine three flavours at once – originally vanilla, strawberry and chocolate. The first recorded tricolour recipe was created by head chef of the Royal Prussian household, Louis Ferdinand Jungius in 1839. In Italy, pistachio replaces chocolate, in tribute to the Italian flag.

Who is the original Mr Whippy? The answer: Dominic Facchino.

After seeing the success of Mr Softee in the U.S., Mr Facchino – an Italian, naturally – began operating the first ice cream trucks in Birmingham, UK in 1958. It was his Mr Whippy that first chimed the iconic ice cream chime, "Greensleeves", now favoured by ice cream vans (along with "O Sole Mio").

Today, according to the BBC, there are just 5,000 operating around the UK.

The Italian word *"gelato"* means "frozen" or "to freeze"*

*The Disney film *Frozen*, weirdly, is not called *Gelato* in Italy.

GERMAN

Bitte mehr eis.

(More ice cream, please.)

America's first ice cream party – a social event solely dedicated to celebrating ice cream – was first recorded in Maryland in 1744. Governor Thomas Bladen indulged his guests with American ice cream. Attendee William Black described it as "fine ice cream".

Glow in the Dark

Charlie Francis, the brains behind the UK-based ice cream maker Lick Me I'm Delicious, has made the world's first glow-in-the-dark ice cream. The ice cream glows when the "synthesized proteins from jellyfish luminescence" are activated, causing the scoops to light up with new each lick.

It costs $200 *a scoop*.

Yes, you read that right.

It's official! According to a recent Japanese study, people who eat ice cream in the morning are more alert and less irritated than those who don't indulge.

However, the ice-cream-loving Japanese also gave the world horse flesh ice cream... so not sure if the data is to be trusted.

Have you ever wondered why milk is white, when it's actually 87 per cent water?

The reason is milkfat – the most important ingredient in ice cream. Fat and protein molecules inside water reflect all light wavelengths, making milk appear white.

Last Meal

Ice cream is the most requested last meal dessert by Death Row inmates in the U.S.

Notoriously, the American terrorist behind the Oklahoma City bombing (and 168 counts of murder), Timothy McVeigh, requested two pints of mint chocolate chip ice cream before his lethal injection. He ate it all.

How To Make Ice Cream

There are 10 steps to making ice cream:

1. Blend together the milkfat source, non-fat solids, stabilizers and emulsifiers.

2. Pasteurize the ice cream mix

3. Homogenize the ice cream mix. to decrease the milkfat globule size for a smoother, creamier ice cream.

4. Age the ice cream mix at 40°F (5°C) overnight.

5. Add flavours and colourings.

6. Freeze and churn the ice cream mix in rotating barrels. (Incorporating air and freezing at the same time is what makes ice cream so fluffy.)*

7. Add any fruits, swirls, nuts, marshmallows.

8. Package.

9. Harden at a temperature of 13°F(-25°C).

10. Eat. Repeat. Sleep.

* It was Nicolas Audiger who in 1674 realized that churning ice cream while slow-freezing ensured a creamier, fluffier texture.

66

In recent months I have developed the habit of stopping off at Will Wright's ice cream parlour for a hot fudge sundae on my way home from my evening drama classes. I'm sure that I couldn't allow myself this indulgence were it not that my normal diet is composed almost totally of protein foods.

99

Marilyn Monroe

For the iconic opening scene of *Breakfast at Tiffany's*, Audrey Hepburn asked the director, Blake Edwards, if she could eat an ice cream cone, instead of a danish. Edwards said no.

But, now imagine that scene with ice cream!

Per capita, the consumption of ice cream in the United States has been decreasing since 2000 up until 2020. In 2020, the average American consumed *just* 12.7 lbs of ice cream when compared to 2000, when it was 16.1 lbs.

According to Statista,

292 million Americans consumed ice cream

in 2020 (out of a possible 350 million).

"

You look like melted ice cream.

"

Rocket Raccoon (To "Fat" Thor),
Avengers: Endgame **(2019)**

"

How about some ice cream? You know, it's stuff that people eat when they're feeling a little down.

"

Sherlock Holmes (Jonny Lee Miller),
Elementary, **2013**

During World War II, it was reported that American soldiers on the ground would mix snow with melted chocolate bars in their helmets to make a sort of chocolate sorbet.

American WWII soldiers loved ice cream. In 1945, the U.S. Navy converted a concrete barge into a floating ice-cream factory. The factory was then towed around the Pacific distributing ice cream to soldiers onboard warships! The floating factory contained more than 2,000 gallons of ice cream and could churn out 10 new gallons every seven minutes.

CHAPTER
FOUR

The Milky Way

Ice cream never disappoints. It's like the Grand Canyon of desserts. And, if you're lucky, just as big. But ice cream is not an island; it is the coming together of many separate elements – milkfat, sugar, cream, eggs, air, and a whole lot of TLC – that combine to create something special. Ice cream is a happy marriage.

Let us now celebrate all these ingredients in unison, and doff our caps to the cows, taste-shakers, and ice cream makers that allow us to eat our just desserts. We salute you...

King Charles II, once an exile in France, returned to his Sceptred Isle with a taste for creamed ice. But he also wanted to keep the recipe a royal secret: ice cream was too good for the commonfolk, he thought (correctly).

So, he paid his ice cream maker to keep schtum and make it only for him. Around 1680, the recipe was leaked by a fellow called Demirco... and a thankful nation has enjoyed it ever since.

Icons of Ice Cream: #2

Founded in 1945 by Burt Baskin and his brother-in-law Irv Robbins in Glendale, California, Baskin-Robbins was famous for its "31 Flavours" marketing slogan, which celebrates a different flavour of ice cream for every day of the month.

Welcome to America

In 1906, immigrants travelling to New York's Ellis Island to start a new life were offered ice cream as part of their first American meal. A rather exhausting New York newspaper headline in 1921 read:

"Ellis Island authorities gently lead immigrants to appreciation of good points of America by introducing

them to the pleasures of ice cream sandwiches."
According to the newspaper, "Some Italian immigrants did not take kindly to the ice cream and they tried to tell officials that they wanted it warmed up." It's estimated that 40 per cent of all Americans today are related to someone who came to America via Ellis Island.

In a 2014 study conducted by Baskin-Robbins, the thought of ice cream puts 72 per cent of respondents in a happy mood, "even if they are stressed or in a serious mood".

Also, the survey reported that 60 per cent of those surveyed are at their happiest, most motivated and inspired when enjoying ice cream with family and friends.

A recent survey revealed that **40 per cent** of Americans have eaten an entire pint of ice cream in one sitting.

February 6, 2023.

National Eat Ice Cream for Breakfast Day.

Happy eating to all those who observe.

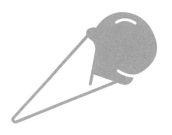

Ice Cream in the UK

According to *The Independent*, in 2021, the UK's favourite flavours were as follows:

1. Vanilla
2. Chocolate
3. Strawberry
4. Mint Choc Chip
5. Salted Caramel
6. Rum and Raisin
7. Pistachio
8. Raspberry
9. Coffee

Three Flavours Cornetto Trilogy

Directed by Edgar Wright, and written by Wright and Simon Pegg, the Three Flavours Cornetto trilogy consists of the now-iconic British movies, *Shaun of the Dead*, *Hot Fuzz*, and *The World's End*. Each film contains a frame of a different colour Cornetto:

Shaun of the Dead – Strawberry Cornetto (represents zombie blood)
Hot Fuzz – Blue original cornetto (represents the police)
At World's End – Green mint chocolate chip (represents the alien's blood)

66

Simon and I contrived to mention Cornettos in each film as a way of getting more free ice cream. We didn't... though we did get some for *The World's End*... two out of three ain't bad.

99

Edgar Wright

"

I'd like a honey
ice cream cone for
me, and a dragonfly
ripple for my friend
the frog.

"

Fozzy Bear, *The Muppet Movie* **(1979)**

ITALIAN

Più gelato, per favore.

(More ice cream, please.)

"

It was like an ice cream cone.

"

Roy Neary (Richard Dreyfus), describing the UFO in *Close Encounters of the Third Kind* (1977)

66

Like love, ice cream gives
us a rush of dopamine, which
is intimately tied to the brain's
reward centre. Ice cream has
two of the ingredients that
we're engineered to have a
big reward response to:
fat and sugar.

99

**Ashley Gearhardt, clinical psychologist
and psychology professor**

How Do You Eat Yours?

There are five main types of ice cream eaters. *Which one are you?*

1. Cycloner: Do you wrap your tongue around the cone and cyclone the ice cream up into your mouth?

2. Biter: Do you bite down on your ice cream and chew it?

3. Hoover: Do you suck the ice cream up like a hoover?

4. Slurper: Do you slow slurp the ice cream through your teeth?

5. Licker: Do you attack the cone with a blizzard of mini licks?

In 2020, according to the Grocer, ice cream lovers in the UK ate an extra 54 million litres of ice cream – **an increase of 20.7 per cent from the previous non-pandemic year.**

66

My name is Joe Biden, and I love ice cream. You all think I'm kidding — I'm not. I eat more ice cream than three other people you'd like to be with, all at once. I don't drink. I don't smoke. But I eat a lot of ice cream.

99

President Joe Biden*

* According to Federal Election Commission data, Joe Biden spent more than $10,000 on Jeni's Splendid Ice Cream (his favourite) while on his 2019 campaign trial towards the White House.

As a 16-year-old, future President Barack Obama worked his first job in a Hawaiian Baskin-Robbins ice cream shop. "Rows and rows of rock-hard ice cream can be brutal on the wrists. And while I may have lost my taste for ice cream after one too many free scoops, I'll never forget that job — or the people who gave me that opportunity — and how they helped me get to where I am today," Obama wrote in his first autobiography.

What Flavour Are You?

According to Dr. Alan Hirsch, in a study for Baskin-Robbins, your favourite ice cream flavour defines who you are:

Vanilla – impulsive, easily suggestible, idealist.

Chocolate – dramatic, lively, charming, flirtatious, seductive.

Strawberry – tolerant, devoted, an introvert.

Mint Chocolate Chip – argumentative, frugal, cautious.

Chocolate Chip Cookie Dough – ambitious, competitive, a visionary.

Pralines 'n Cream – loving, supportive, and prefer to avoid the spotlight.

Butter Pecan – devoted, conscientious, respectful.

Jamoca – scrupulous, conscientious, a moral perfectionist.

Chocolate Chip – generous, competent, a go-getter.

Rainbow Sherbet – analytic, decisive, pessimistic.

Rocky Road – aggressive, engaging, a good listener.

Coffee – dramatic, thrive on passion, and in need of constant stimulation.

As reported in *Time*, in 2017, during his tenure as president, **Donald Trump insisted that he have two scoops of ice cream** on top of his chocolate cream pie (his preferred dessert), **while those joining him at his table were allowed just one scoop.**

In 1850, there were only 20 ice cream places where one could buy ice cream in the UK. At the time, few were convinced the creamed ice craze would take off. Henry Mayhew, an esteemed Victorian journalist and founder of *Punch* magazine, recalled hearing one ice cream vendor say: "Lord, I've seen people splutter when they taste ice cream for the first time, as I much did myself. They get among the teeth and they make you feel as if your tooth ached all over."

"

Without ice cream, there would be darkness and chaos.

"

Don Kardong

> 66

Tomorrow, we can eat broccoli, but today is for ice cream.

> 99

Malory Hobson

New Zealand –

the world's largest consumer of ice cream, incredibly – have their very own unofficial ice cream flavour: The Hokey Pokey. Plain vanilla ice cream mixed with small chunks of honeycomb toffee. All together now, "Oh...hokey pokey pokey..."

According to Instacart, vanilla is the most purchased ice cream flavour in every U.S. state, accounting for **more than 26.2 per cent of all ice cream sales in the U.S.**

CHAPTER
FIVE

Churn Baby Churn

Ice cream was not invented overnight. Its journey from basic fruit-flavoured ice to highly evolved chunky-monkey-hokey-pokey-knickerbocker-supercallifragulisticexpealidous-sundae has been a multitude of micro-invention. Today, we are spoiled with hundreds-and-thousands of flavours, but that's not always been the case. So, let us now bow our heads and pray for the poor souls who never lived to taste Mint-Choc-Chip.

On June 13, 1789, Elizabeth Hamilton – the wife of Alexander Hamilton (the first Secretary of the Treasury of the United States) – first served ice cream to the newly-appointed President George Washington. The ice cream was the highlight of the dinner party, and from then on Washington began serving it at a future events at the White House.

According to the
IDFA, in 1790, George
Washington spent $200*
on ice cream during his
first year as president.
Favours for flavours?

*(That's more than $5,000 in today's money!)

"

Don't let your
ice cream melt
while you're
counting someone
else's sprinkles.

"

Akilah Hughes

In Roald Dahl's *Charlie and the Chocolate Factory* (1964), Willy Wonka's fiercest rival, Fickelgruber, stole Wonka's invention for the never-melting ice cream.

As a result, Wonka fired his staff, closed the factory doors...and hired the mysterious Oompa Loompas.

Knickerbocker Glory

Want to make a Knickerbocker glory? Of course you do.

• Squeeze a generous squirt of chocolate syrup at the base of a tall sundae glass.
• Dollop in three scoops of vanilla ice cream, alternating with a layer of fresh fruit before each scoop.
• Top with lots of squirty whipped cream.
• Add a cherry on top. *Et voila!*

I never in my life argued with a bowl of ice cream.

Ray Bradbury

The now-iconic phrase "I Scream, You Scream, We All Scream for Ice Cream" derives from a song of the same name, first released in 1927.

Written by Howard Johnson, Billy Moll, and Robert A. King, the song, once deemed a novelty song, is now a huge part of U.S. popular culture, and a jazz standard.

FRENCH

Plus de glace s'il vous plait.

(More ice cream, please.)

Spaghetti Ice Cream

A German delicacy, *spaghettieis*, or spaghetti ice cream, was invented by Dario Fontanella in 1969. He was the first (maybe) to squeeze vanilla ice cream through a spaghetti press. Today, it's estimated that more than 25 million bowls of spaghettieis are sold every year in Germany.

Más helado por favor.

(More ice cream, please.)

When in Rome do as the Italians do and mix business with pleasure. Order an **_Affogato al caffe_** - a shot of espresso poured over a scoop of ice cream.

"Affogato" means "drowned" in Italian.

Icons of Ice Cream: #3

Created in 1961 by Reuben and Rose Mattus in New York, Häagen-Dazs is one of the world's most beloved luxury ice cream brands. They opened their first store on November 15, 1976 in Brooklyn. Today, there are more than 900 Häagen-Dazs icream shops in 50 countries.

Banana Split

Perhaps the greatest American invention of all time, the Banana Split* is the height of healthy ice cream innovation. To make your own:

• Peel a banana and, most importantly, split it down the centre lenghtways. Pop it in a bowl.

• Add three scoops of ice cream on top.

• Then squirt on your personal choice of the following: whipped cream, fruit syrup or chocolate or fudge sauce, chopped nuts.
• Add a cherry on top.

*The Banana Split was invented in 1904 by an optometrist named David Strickler in Latrobe, Pennsylvania.

Ice Cream Float

Also known as a coke float, or ice cream soda float, the Float is ingenious in its simplicity: ice cream drenched in fizzy soda. It was invented by Robert McCay Green in Philadelphia, in 1874, after he ran out of whipped cream. So, he just poured soda on.

During Prohibition (1920–1929), ice cream floats became America's most sought-after guilty pleasure.

"

Monogamy is like saying you're never gonna have any other ice cream flavour besides rocky road.

"

Dr Greg House (Hugh Laurie), *House*, Season 5, Episode 16: "The Softer Side"

66

I smell ice cream. They've got pralines and cream, they've got Mississippi mud, and they got chocolate eruption, and they got apple, and they got grape. They got grape, and super-duper chocolate eruption, and...

99

Chunk (Jeff Cohen), *The Goonies* (1985)

Neuroscientists at the Institute of Psychiatry have recently published articles that prove that eating ice cream lights up the orbitofrontal cortex of the brain, the same pleasure-processing centre that gets excited when people win money or listen to their favourite music.

In a nationwide U.S. Dairy Foods survey, **45 per cent** said that ice cream is their favourite indulgence.

According to the Guinness
World Records, the world's
largest scoop of ice cream
weighed a whopping

1,365kg
(3,010 lb)

– the same weight as a
female hippo – when it was
scooped on June 28, 2014,
in Cedarburg, Wisconsin.

Ben & Jerry's
10 Bestselling Flavours 2021

Cookie Dough
Chocolate Fudge Brownie
Phish Food
Caramel Chew
Karamel Sutra
Cookie Dough Sandwich
Cookie Dough S'wich Up
Topped Salted Caramel Brownie
Peanut Butter Cup
Half Baked

Every year, Ben & Jerry's receive more than 13,000 flavour suggestions from fans. (They claim to read them all – "even the really weird ones".)

The legendary *Godfather* actor, Marlon Brando, was known to devour a whole tub of vanilla and/or rum-raisin ice cream every night. He adored ice cream. During the filming of the now-famous *Mutiny on the Bounty* (1962), Brando split 52 pairs of tight-fitting breeches and would often leave the set, even when they were filming, to go sit in a canoe with a tub of ice cream. Thankfully, the film was shot in widescreen.

According to the Guinness World Records, the most ice cream scoops balanced on a cone is 125! This tall-but-true feat was achieved by Italian, Dimitri Panciera in Rome, Italy, on November 17, 2018.

Bassetts Ice Cream
is America's oldest
ice cream company.
This fifth-generation
business has been
serving up the cold stuff
in Philadelphia since
1861, when batches of
ice cream were churned
by mule power.

CHAPTER
SIX

Cherry On Top

Uh-oh. We've hit the bottom of the tub. What a bittersweet ending – so good, and yet maybe you've over-indulged. If you've got the "ice cream sweats" (you know, when you can feel ice cream on your lungs from eating a lot), then apologies, we've treated you too much. Let us cleanse your palate with one final lick, and then you can go for a well-deserved lie down.

Funfetti!

Sprinkles were invented in 1913 by Erven H. de Jong from Wormerveer. They were named

hagelslag

after their resemblance to hail, a prominent wet-weather feature in the Netherlands.

According to the Guinness World Records, the most ice cream eaten in one minute was two pint tubs of Ben & Jerry's Strawberry Cheesecake! Australian Isaac Harding-Davis devoured the challenge in Sydney, Australia on July 16, 2017.

Icons of Ice Cream: #4

The original soft-serve ice cream man-and-van brand, Mister Softee, first opened its doors to customers in Philadelphia in 1956, and was founded by John Conway. The first ice cream cones cost just 10 cents. Today, Mister Softee is the largest franchisor of soft-serve in the U.S., with a fleet of 625 trucks.

A la mode:

When the French say *A la mode* it means "in the style of". In the U.S., however, *A la mode* refers to a dessert (usually a slice of pie) served with a scoop of ice cream on top.

According to a recent study
on the neurological effects of
food, researchers found that ice
cream lowers the human startle
response in men and women.
**People stuffed with ice cream
are less likely to feel scared.**
The phenomenon, it appears, is largely
psychological, a result of the learned
associations pairing ice cream with
safe childhood home memories.

Before 1900, in America, women were not allowed to eat in restaurants unless accompanied by a man. Before long, thankfully, eateries started popping up to offer women a place to eat that was genteel and ladylike, a place befitting their femininity. And definitely not a bar. These places were affectionately dubbed **"ice cream saloons"**.

Most ice cream historians agree that the first ever ice cream parlour originated in France around 1686. Founded by Francesco Procopio del Coltelli, Paris' first café, called Café Procope, was also the first to serve gelato to the sticky-fingered French public. Its success gave rise to the *gelateria*, an ice cream shop that serves Italian-style ice cream.

America's Sweethearts

According to the International Dairy Foods Association, these were the U.S.'s most popular ice cream flavours in 2021:

Vanilla
Chocolate
Cookies N' Cream
Mint Chocolate Chip
Chocolate Chip Cookie Dough
Buttered Pecan
Cookie Dough
Strawberry
Fudge
Neapolitan

While Italians today take all the credit (deservedly so) for the beauty of modern milky creamed ice, it was the Chinese who first started the ice cream craze with, well, frozen yoghurt. During the Tang Dynasty (A.D. 618–907), in China, Buffalo, cows' and goats' milk was heated, fermented, thickened and refrigerated underground. It would be another millennia before milk-based ice creams were introduced to Europe in the tenth century.

The International Dairy Foods Association estimates the global ice cream market will reach a sales volume value of a whopping **$91.9 billion by 2027, a 30 per cent increase from $70.9 billion in 2019**, and almost the same size as the global coffee demand.

66

Being married means I can break wind and eat ice cream in bed.

99

Brad Pitt

66

That was the best
ice cream soda I
ever tasted.

99

**Lou Costello
(his now-famous last words –
he died immediately after)**

"

There is no sincerer love than the love of ice cream.

"

George Bernard Shaw

"

A day without ice cream was a day wasted.

"

Iain Pears

66

We dare not trust our wit for making our house pleasant to our friend, so we buy ice cream.

99

Ralph Waldo Emerson

According to the
Guinness World Records,
the world's tallest ice
cream cone measured
3.08m (10ft 1.26in.)
in height, the same height
as a basketball hoop. The
feat was accomplished by two
Norweigians, Hennig-Olsen
and Trond L. Wøien, in
Norway, on July 26, 2015.

66

She could not have
gazed at him with
a more rapturous
intensity if she had
been a small child
and he a saucer of
ice cream.

P. G. Wodehouse

According to the Guinness World Records, Allan Ganz, resident of Peabody, Massachusetts, has the longest continuous career working as an ice cream man. **67 years from 1947 to 2014.**

"

I go running when I have to. When the ice cream truck is doing sixty.

"

Wendy Liebman

66

My love for ice
cream emerged
at an early age —
and never left!

99

Ginger Rogers

66

I think the serving size of ice cream is when you hear the spoon hit the bottom of the container.

99

Brian Regan